# BIRDS ALPHABET
## COLORING BOOK

### RUTH SOFFER

**DOVER PUBLICATIONS, INC.**
Mineola, New York

*Bibliographical Note*

*Birds Alphabet Coloring Book* is a new work, first published by Dover
Publications, Inc., in 2005.

DOVER *Pictorial Archive* SERIES

*International Standard Book Number: 0-486-44035-4*

Manufactured in the United States of America
Dover Publications, Inc., 31 East 2nd Street, Mineola, N.Y. 11501

# PUBLISHER'S NOTE

Birds come in many different shapes, sizes, and colors. Found in every corner of the globe, they are an important part of the natural order: birds control insect populations, help pollinate plants and flowers, and fill woods, gardens, suburban backyards, and city windowsills with song and movement. Birds are the only animals with feathers, and because of their ability to fly, they have colonized the whole world—from the icy wastes of Antarctica to steaming jungles and barren deserts. In all, there are over 9,000 species of birds.

In this coloring book you'll find a bird for each letter of the alphabet, along with three additional species, ranging from such familiar visitors as the robin, bluebird, and junco, to the toucan, xenops, and resplendent quetzal—beautiful birds found in tropical rain forests. Use colored pencils, crayons, felt-tip pens, and other media to color these detailed, accurate drawings of both familiar and lesser-known birds of the world.

With a little research and study, youngsters and nature lovers alike can make the twenty-nine birds in this collection come to vivid, glowing life. This book will also reinforce letter-recognition skills among younger readers, as well as stimulate interest in bird life and the natural world in general. (See p. 32 for a complete list of the birds in this book.)

**A is for Avocet**
(American, *Recurvirostra americana*)

**B is for Bluebird**
(Eastern, *Sialia sialis*)
Far left: Female

**C is for Cardinal**
*( Richmondena cardinalis )*
Upper right: Female

**D is for Duck**
(Female mallard, *Anas platyrhynchos*)

**E is for Egret**
(Snowy, *Egretta thula*)

**F is for Flicker**
(Northern, *Colaptes auratus*)

**G is for Goldfinch**
(American, *Carduelis tristis*)

**H is for Hummingbird**
(Ruby-throated, *Archilochus colubris*)

**I is for Ibis**
(Glossy, *Plegadis falcinellus*)

**J is for Junco**
(Dark-eyed, *Junco hyemalis*)

**K is for Kingfisher**
(Belted, *Ceryle alcyon*)

**L is for Lovebirds**
(Peachfaced, *Agapornis roseicollis*)

15

**Cedar Waxwing**
(*Bombycilla cedrorum*)

**Wilson's Warbler**
(*Wilsonia pusilla*)

**Cedar Waxwing**
(*Bombycilla cedrorum*)

**Rose-breasted Grosbeak**
(*Pheucticus ludovicianus*)

17

**M is for Mockingbird**
(Northern, *Mimus polyglottos*)

**N is for Nuthatch**

Top: Red-breasted Nuthatch *(Sitta canadensis)*
Bottom: White-breasted Nuthatch *(Sitta carolinensis)*

**O is for Oriole**

(Northern, *Icterus galbula*)

**P is for Painted Bunting**

*(Passerina ciris)*

**Q is for Quetzal**

(Resplendent, *Pharomachrus mocinno*)

Bottom left: Female

**R is for Robin**
(American, *Turdus migratorius*)

**S is for Swan**

(Mute, *Cygnus olor*)

**T is for Toucan**
Left: Chestnut-mandibled *( Ramphastos swainsonii)*
Right: White-breasted *( Ramphastos vitellinus)*

25

**U is for Umbrella Bird**

*(Cephalopterus ornatus)*

**V is for Vireo**

(Red-eyed, *Vireo olivaceus*)

**W is for Warbler**
(Myrtle, *Dendroica coronata*)

**X is for Xenops**

*(Xenops minutus)*

**Y is for Yellowthroat**
(Common, *Geothlypis trichas*)

**Z is for Zebra Finch**
(*Poephila castanotis*)

# LIST OF BIRDS

Page